Acknowledgement of Land & of the Traditional Owners of this Land

I would like to acknowledge the Gadigal people of the Eora Nation, upon whose stolen land I stand on today.

I recognise that this land was never terra nullius — the land belonging to these peoples was never ceded, given up, bought or sold.

I would like to pay my respects to Aboriginal Elders past, present and emerging, and I extend this acknowledgement to all Aboriginal and Torres Strait Islander people.

This book is dedicated to my uncle "Zio" Tonino.
He had a tragic, sad & lonely life.

"The Don"
December, 2020

Antonio Martone
San Fele, Potenza, Basilicata, Italy
(1947-2020)

Foreword

"Don" Vito is a poet, non-conformist. Delicate in the feeling of the word, but not mushy in the sense of life. It is authentic, canny, unconventional. Standards? No. They don't dictate it. "The Don" creates them. The ferocious tongue is with one who is limited to minimizing the beauty of life.

Don is well aware that what is lived and not posted is the true grace of life. In Love, a true "Don Juan", wise in choosing his conquests, as the heart dictates the poems he recites.

The elders were right: only the wise are encouraged to live life. Fools, when faced with mishaps, flee from it like fearful, overwhelmed, boring boys and girls. Don, don't. He turns the bale into milk and honey.

Manna from heaven are the sweetened verses, however, with a hint of sin, that from their fist, winged, run in haste to come to life.

This collection of poems is, without a doubt, the real proof that, really beautiful, it is the one who sees the world through conventional eyes, but with the eyes of poetry.

Danielle Abrantes
18.09.2020

E-mail: daniapc10@yahoo.com.br
https://www.resilienciamag.com/author/danieledepaula/

Contents

1: Marijuana
(Mary Jane)
2: The Third Eye
(Tertia Oculus)
3: Let's Get Stoned
4: Absurdity
5: Toxic Love
6: Submission
(Sottomissione)
7: Transformation
(Trasformazione)
8: Jessie Cool
9: The Man in Black
(L'homme en Noir)
10: Planet Earth
(Planète Terre)
11: Confusion
(Confusione)
12: The Future
(Il Futuro)
13: Dangerous Ideas
(Idées Dangereuses)
14: Cook Was a Killer
(Terra Nullis)
15: Questions
16: The Twilight Zone
17: Space, the Final Frontier
18: The Manhattan Project
19: The Cosmos
20: Nemesis
21: Perseverance
(Persévérance)
22: Numerology
23: The Power of the Atom
24: Fire
(Fuoco)
25: Pleasure & Pain

Contents

26: Namaste
27: Operation Buffalo
(Maralinga)
28: How to Make Relationships Work
29: GFE
(Girlfriend Experience)
30: Lo♥e In A Cold Climate
(Amore in un Clima Freddo)
31: Born to be Wild
32: Lo♥e?
33: Pussy Power
34: Thinking
(Pensiero)
35: Black Beauty
36: Nose Bleed
37: Subjectivity
38: It's Not Either Or
39: Angry Poetry
(The Anti-Virus)
40: What is Life?
41: La Dolce Vita
(The Sweet Life)
42: *(I Want to be)* Marcello Mastroianni
43: Rantings of a Madman
(Discorso di un Pazzo)
44: Bottle of Wine
(Bottiglia di Vino)
45: The Legend of Jonah Lomou
46: In the Garden of Eden
(In a Gadda da Vida)
47: In the Garden of Perdition
(In a Gadda da Petition)
48: HerStory
49: The Times They Are NOT A-Changin'
50: Death is the Price You Pay for Living

Marijuana
(Mary Jane)

Marijuana, Marijuana.
Embrace me in your sweet aroma.
Envelope me in your warm embrace.
Hold me in your tender bosom.
Kiss me with your sweet lips.

Mary Jane, Mary Jane.
I call out you name.
You always answer my call.
You never disappoint me.
You always go straight to my soul.

Mary Jane, Mary Jane.
Marijuana by another name.
We've known each for a very long time.
We've never had an argument.
You never made feel bad.

Marijuana, Marijuana.
You've been mistreated.
You've been misunderstood.
You've been outlawed.
You're just doin' what you should.

You stand so tall & proud.
With your leaves & seeds so resplendent.
You contain mystical, transformative powers.
You play with the mind.
You, open portals to other Realities.

You make one see what cannot be seen.
You make one feel what cannot be felt.
You make one think what cannot be thought.
You make one imagine what cannot be imagined.

For this you are condemned.
Your reputation sullied.
Your powers ridiculed.
Your fame notorious.
Your legacy tarnished.
Your natural integrity without artificial additions.

But now people are being to see.
The true gifts that you provide to all.
The medicinal powers that you possess.
To cure cancers, pain & stress.
You are finally being seen for what you really are.
Are part of Nature, like everything else.

"The Don"
29.06.202

The Third Eye
(Tertia Oculus)

You think you can see.
You think you know where you are.
You think you know *"Reality"*.
You think that your eyes are wide open.
You think that what you see is all there is.
You think that's all to see.

There is another eye that you possess.
It lets you see what you cannot see.
It lets you see with your eyes closed.
It lets you see inside your heart.
It lets you see into your soul.
It's called *The Third Eye*.

It lies in the middle of your forehead.
It lies inside your mind.
It is your spiritual eye.
It can see what your two other eyes cannot.
It can see infinity.
It can see beyond imagination.
It can see outside Space & Time.
It exists in a dimension of its own.

The Third Eye cannot be opened easily.
You have to learn how to unlock its mysteries.
You have to learn how to access doorway.
You have to learn how to use the access code.
You have to master its key.

Search for the *"Keeper of the Key"*.
Search out the *"Ancient Knowledge"*.
This *"Knowledge"* has been around for an eternity.
Lost because of stupidity of man.
This *"Knowledge"* is still there.
Ready to be rediscovered.
By someone, like you, ready to study & to learn.

The rewards will be unimaginable.
The things you will see.
It will blow your tiny mind.
It will change your *"Reality"*.
It will make see things like never before.
You will not be the same person, that you were before.
When you see with your *The Third Eye*.

It's your *"Mind's Eye"*.
It's your *"Inner Eye"*.
Maybe, it's *"God's Eye"*?
Maybe, it's the *"Devil's Eye"*?
Maybe, it's the *"Demon's Eye"*?
Maybe, it's the *"Eye of Horus"*?
Maybe, it's the *"Eye of Ra"*?
Maybe, it's the *"Eye of Osiris*?
Maybe it's the *"Eye of Isis"*?
Maybe it's the *"Pineal Gland"*?
It definitely is, your *Third Eye*.

Tertia Oculus

(The Third Eye)

"The Don"
29.06.2020

Let's Get Stoned

Let's get stoned.
Let's get high.
Let's forget all of our worries.
Let's leave this cruel world.
Let's leave "Reality" behind.
Let's create a new world.
Let's open a portal into another dimension.

This World is not working for me.
It ain't doing me any good.
"Reality" never lived up to what it cracked up to be.
"Reality" never really did anything for me.
Fantasy & Illusion always seemed more appealing.
They offered more adventure & fun.
With less pain & suffering.
More loving & happiness.

My recommendation, to anyone that wants to listen, is:
Let's all get stoned.
Let's all get out of this madness.
Let's escape to another place.
Let's leave all this bullshit behind us.
Let's all start again.

A place where there are no politicians.
Where there are no Leaders.
Where money doesn't exist.
Where violence has no meaning.
Where borders are non-existent.
Where Nations co-exist.
Where people live together.
Where there is respect for each other.
Where there is love & harmony.

This place does exist.
This place is in my mind.
This place I can go to any time.
This place is always open, 24/7.
This place is called "Nirvana".
This place is called "The Promised Land".

It's easy to get to.
The road is straight & true.
It's down "Highway 61".
Just up from "Route 66".
Just around the corner from "Roadhouse Blues".
Just close to "Heartbreak Hotel".
Get some dinner at "Alice's Restaurant".
Meet me at the "5 & Dime, Jimmy Dean, Jimmy Dean".
But whatever you do don't stay at "Hotel California".
Because you can "check out anytime you like but you can never leave".
It's just a matter of checking into the "Chelsea Hotel".
With my old pal Leonard Cohen.
Then, let's get stoned.

Let's Get Stoned

"The Don"
29.06.2030

Absurdity

Don't complain to me.
Don't climb up a tree.
Don't just let it be.
Don't try to be free.
Don't even try to see.
'Cause it's all Absurdity.

Don't question your situation.
Don't complain about the state of the nation.
Don't talk about objectification.
Don't come to any realisation.
Don't mention the commercialisation.
'Cause it's all Absurdity.

Don't jump up & down.
Don't try to be a clown.
Don't fret or wear a frown.
Don't take off your gown.
Don't trust any crown.
'Cause it's all Absurdity.

Don't use your imagination.
Don't go into hibernation.
Don't seek liberation.
Don't try to work out the combination.
Don't enjoy any fornication.
'Cause it's all Absurdity.

Don't seek any solution.
Don't try to solve your confusion.
Don't come to any conclusion.
Don't try to understand Nuclear Fusion.
Don't seek out retribution.
'Cause it's all Absurdity.

Don't seek amnesty
Don't look for eternity.
Don't search for security.
Don't think it's just a travesty.
Don't lose faith in Humanity.
'Cause it's all Absurdity.

"The Don"
30.06.2020

Toxic Love

It's abusive love.
It's refusal love.
It's not mutual love.
It's second hand love.
It's hurtful love.
It's possessive love.
It's jealous love.
It's unhealthy love.
It's unfriendly love.
It's uncaring love.
It's non-sharing love.
It's lying love.
It's a suffering love.
It's not a two-way love.
It's a destructive love.
It's an enslaving love.
It's psychotic love.
It's myopic love.
It's traumatic love.
It's poisonous love.
It's submissive love.
It's manipulative love.
It's humiliation love.
It's belittling love.
It's conflictive love.
It's hypocritical love.
It's painful love.
It's violent love.
It's not love.
It's fake love.

"The Don"
30.06.2020

Submission

(Sottomissione)

Submit to my Will.
Submit to my Power.
Submit to my Desire.
Submit to my Fire.
Submit to my Pleasure.

Submit be my Treasure.
Submit be my Slave.
Submit be my Bitch.
Submit be my Goofer.
Submit be my Loafer.

Submit & make me happy.
Submit & make me laugh.
Submit & make me come.
Submit & make me glad.
Submit & make me bad.

Submit to my every need.
Submit to my every want.
Submit to my every vice.
Submit to my every craving.
Submit to my every perversion.

Submit to your place.
Submit to your position.
Submit to your situation.
Submit to your condition.
Submit to your prison.

Submission is our situation.
Submission is our position.
Submission is our only choice.
Submission is our only decision.
Submission is our Life.

Submission or Death.

"The Don"
30.06.2020

Transformation

(Trasformazione)

Transform yourself.
Reform yourself.
Enlighten yourself.
Illuminate yourself.
Sacrifice yourself.
Praise yourself.
Prioritise yourself.
Educate yourself.
Teach yourself
Illustrate yourself.
Question yourself.
Don't double guess yourself.
Reach into yourself.
Feel deep within yourself.
Laugh at yourself.
Forgive yourself.
Relax yourself.
Destress yourself.
Fuck yourself.
Destroy yourself.
Be true to yourself.
Be at Peace with yourself.
Centre yourself.
Align yourself.
Lose yourself.
Find yourself.
Harmonise yourself.
Love yourself.
Humanise yourself.

"The Don"
30.06.2020

Jessie Cool

Jessie Cool, Jessie Cool.
Cool Jessie, cool, cool Jessie.

Jessie Cool, Jessie Cool.
Cool Jessie, cool, cool Jessie.

Jessie Cool, Jessie Coooooool.
Jessie Cool, Jessie Cool.

Cool Jessie, cool, cool Jessie.
Cool Jessie, cool, cool Jessie.

She was still at school.
Cool Jessie, cool, cool Jessie.
Cool Jessie, cool, cool Jessie.

When I met her by the pool.
Cool Jessie, cool, cool Jessie.
Cool Jessie, cool, cool Jessie.

I began to drooooooool.
Cool Jessie, cool, cool Jessie.
Cool Jessie, cool, cool Jessie.

Jessie Cool, Jessie Cool.
Cool Jessie, cool, cool Jessie.

Jessie Cool, Jessie Coooooool.
Jessie Cool, Jessie Cool.

Jessie Cool, Jessie Cool.
Cool Jessie, cool, cool Jessie.

She came over to the bar.
Cool Jessie, cool, cool Jessie.
Cool Jessie, cool, cool Jessie.

I was playing my guitar.
Jessie Cool, Jessie Cool.
Cool Jessie, cool, cool Jessie.

I said, "We could go faaaaaaar".
Jessie Cool, Jessie Cool.
Cool Jessie, cool, cool Jessie.

Jessie Cool, Jessie Cool.
Cool Jessie, cool, cool Jessie.

Jessie Cool, Jessie Cool.
Cool Jessie, cool, cool Jessie.

Jessie Cool, Jessie Coooooool.
Jessie Cool, Jessie Cool.

Cool Jessie, cool, cool Jessie.
Cool Jessie, cool, cool Jessie.

I said, "Do you wanna go for a ride?"
Jessie Cool, Jessie Cool.
Cool Jessie, cool, cool Jessie.

"We could go & hide".
Jessie Cool, Jessie Cool.
Cool Jessie, cool, cool Jessie.

"You could stay by my siiiiiiiiiide".
Jessie Cool, Jessie Cool.
Cool Jessie, cool, cool Jessie.

Jessie Cool, Jessie Cool.
Cool Jessie, cool, cool Jessie.

Jessie Cool, Jessie Cool.
Cool Jessie, cool, cool Jessie.

Jessie Cool, Jessie Coooooool.
Jessie Cool, Jessie Cool.

Cool Jessie, cool, cool Jessie.
Cool Jessie, cool, cool Jessie.

Now, we're in Love.
Jessie Cool, Jessie Cool.
Cool Jessie, cool, cool Jessie.

Like two sweet little doves.
Jessie Cool, Jessie Cool.
Cool Jessie, cool, cool Jessie.

We fit like a hand in a gloooooooooove.
Jessie Cool, Jessie Cool.
Cool Jessie, cool, cool Jessie.

Jessie Cool, Jessie Cool.
Cool Jessie, cool, cool Jessie.

Jessie Cool, Jessie Coooooool.
Jessie Cool, Jessie Cool.

Cool Jessie, cool, cool Jessie.
Cool Jessie, cool, cool Jessie.

Cool Jessie, cool, cool Jessie.
Cool Jessie, cool, cool Jessie.

"The Don"
30.06.2020

The Man in Black

(L'homme en Noir)

He wears the colour black.
As constant reminder.
So, that we will never forget.
So, that it's always in our face.
That it's always in our mind.
Of all the atrocities carried out by mankind.

All the injustices.
All the cruelty.
All the abuses.
All the tragedies.
All the disempowerment.
All the disenfranchised.
All the stolen peoples.
All the exploited.
All the exploitation.
All the destruction.
All the downtrodden.
All the poverty.
All the loneliness.
All the fake truths.
All the lies.
All the greediness.
All the deceptions.
All the despair.
All the poverty.
All the inequalities.
All the discrimination.
All the suicides.
All the killings.
All the deaths.
All the wars.
All the violence.
All the inhumanity.
All the Dead on this planet, called Earth.

That's what the man in black says.
With that colour on his back.

"The Don"
01.07.2020

Planet Earth
(Planète Terre)

Plenty for of land to make a home.
Plenty of homes to make a village.
Plenty of Villages to make a town.
Plenty of towns to make a city.
Plenty of cities to make a nation.

Plenty of people to make a community.
Plenty of communities to make a culture.
Plenty of cultures to make a society.
Plenty of societies to make a world.
Plenty of worlds for everyone.

Plenty of land to grow food.
Plenty of food for our mouths.
Plenty of mouths on all the children.
Plenty of children without food.
Plenty of food to feed everyone.

Plenty of land to build a home.
Plenty of homes if you have money.
Plenty of money if there was equality.
Plenty of equality if there was fairness.
Plenty of fairness if we had a heart.

Plenty of laws yet so many justices.
Plenty of injustices faced by people.
Plenty of people with suffering.
Plenty of suffering, too much pain.
Plenty of pain for too many people.

Plenty of voices shout out in protests.
Plenty of protests take to the streets.
Plenty of streets in every city.
Plenty of cities show their opposition.
Plenty of opposition to those People in Power.

Plenty of lives have been killed for no reason.
Plenty of reason to be full of anger & rage.
Plenty of rage against discrimination.
Plenty of discrimination in our lives.
Plenty of lives are abused & exploited.
Plenty exploited are starting a Revolution.

Plenty live in hopelessness & despair.
Plenty of despair & inequality.
Plenty of inequality, violence & wars.
Plenty of senseless wars & destruction.
Plenty of destruction throughout all lands.
Plenty of lands to make things right.

This is Planet Earth!

"The Don"
01.07.2020

Confusion

(Confusione)

There's confusion everywhere.
There's uncertainty in the air.
There's fear in my heart.
There's a revolution & it's about to start.

Are you with us or against us?
Don't hesitate & get on the bus.
It's the strong or the dead.
It's be a leader or be led.

Things are moving quickly that's for sure.
It's now or never, it's not like before.
The situation is serious, gotta make a move.
Come on baby, quick, get with the groove.

The times they are a'changin'.
Everything is rearrangin'.
Politicians are getting greedy.
There's no food to feed the needy.

Fat cats are getting richer.
There's unrest in the picture.
Too many people are disillusioned.
Their lives are being ruined.

Time to for action, time to make a stand.
Time to take control, time to join the band.
Time to get rid of the old & put in the young.
Time to give back *"The Power"* to everyone.

It's time for *"Real"* Democracy to be put in place.
Not this sham & *"Fake"* one that is shoved in our face.
Everything's changing, so don't stand still.
I'll meet you when it's all over, up on top of the hill.

There's political upheaval everywhere.
In every Nation, it's in the air.
There's disillusionment with our so called *"leaders"*, throughout the population.
We're gonna get rid of them, once & for all & write a *"Declaration for a new Nation"*!

"The Don"
02.07.2020

The Future
(Il Futuro)

This World is burning, burning.
This Earth is burning, burning.
This Country is burning, burning.
This Nation is burning, burning.
This Sky is burning, burning.
This Land is burning, burning.
This sea is burning, burning.
This forest is burning, burning.
This soil is burning, burning.
This animal is burning, burning.
This hand is burning, burning.
This eye is burning, burning.
This mind is burning, burning.
This heart is burning, burning.
This soul is burning, burning.
This person is burning, burning.
This Life is burning, burning.
This greed is burning, burning.
This Poverty is burning, burning.
This Inequality is burning, burning.
This Discrimination is burning, burning.
This Hypocrisy is burning, burning.
This Environment is burning, burning.
This Government is burning, burning.
This Establishment is burning, burning.
This Leader is burning, burning.
This Monarchy is burning, burning.
This Patriarchy is burning, burning.
This Democracy is burning, burning.
This Society is burning, burning.
This House is burning, burning.
This **Future** is burning, burning.

"The Don"
03.07.2020

Dangerous Ideas

(Idées Dangereuses)

Don't have thoughts.
Don't have feelings.
Don't have opinions.
Don't have a voice.
Don't have eyes.
Don't have ears.
Don't have arms.
Don't have legs.
Don't have a mind.
Don't have a soul.
Don't have a heart.
Don't have imagination.
Don't have humanity.
Don't have kindness.
Don't have Lo♥e.
Don't have caring.
Don't have nurturing.
Don't have education.
Don't have an environment.
Don't have rights.
Don't have a vote
Don't have Freedom.
Don't have Peace.
Don't have a planet.
Don't have The Truth.
Don't have integrity.
Don't have ethics.
Don't have morality.
Don't have "Dangerous Ideas"!

"The Don"
05.07.2020

Cook Was a Killer

(Terra Nullis)

He claims he found *"The Great South Land"*.
But all he did was lie & kill.
He claimed it was inhabited.
Of course, it was a lie.
First Nations Peoples had been long ago.
For 120,000 years or more.
Nobody really knows for sure.

He claimed for the *"White"* man.
The evil & cruel British Empire.
All it was concerned about colonising.
Exploiting other lands.
Spreading vermin & diseases.
Ruining other pristine lands.

He called it *"Terra Australis"*.
A wild unkept land.
Denied the existence
Of the oldest living culture.
Throughout any lands.
Claimed it for the King.
As though it was theirs to take.

He said it was *"Terra Nullis"*.
Meaning *"empty land"*.
This meant they were free
To come & destroy this land.
To spread their religion.
Of God, good & bad & suffering.
Steeling children from their mothers.
"The Stolen Generation".

Cook was a killer.
He was not a hero to be admired.
Let's put the record straight.
Let's write the *"real"* history.
The history of The First Nations Peoples.
Whose land was stolen from them.
Their culture & their sacred sites desecrated.
Treated like slaves in their own land.
Denied of any human rights.

Cook was a killer!
Don't be fooled by the lies.
When he sailed into Botany Bay.
Back in 1770 like Gods.
The first thing he did.
Was to shoot an Aborigine dead.

They called it the *"firing stick"*.
But we know what it was.
Let's call it for what it is.
A shotgun!
They only had boomerangs & spears
How could they compete.
It was a fair fight.
It was never meant to be.

Cook was a killer!
Let's bring down his statues.
Let's say how it was.
Let's not idolise him.
Like the *"White"* people do.
Let's state the facts.
Cook was a killer & that is a fact!

He was killed in *"The Sandwich Islands"*.
By his own knife he had gifted to one of the warriors.
On February 14, 1779.
Now known as the *"Island of Hawaii"*.
By the Indigenous People of the land.
He was attempting to kidnap their King, *"Kalani'opu'u"*.
Apparently, to reclaim a stolen cutter from one of his ships.
A battle ensued & many warriors were killed.

They cut him up into little pieces.
Boiled him in pot.
Striped his flesh from his bones.
They believed that the power of a man was in his bones.
And left him out to rot.
They knew that they were wrong.
When, they thought he was a *"God"*.
Instead he was a mortal man.
And an *"evil"* one at that.

"Have a good life, so you can have a good Death!", that's what I say.
Does the nature of one's death tell us anything of their life?
Does the way a man died, tell us anything of what type of man he was?
I think it does!

When they first saw the sails of the *"Discovery"*.
The first *"white man"* they'd ever seen.
They thought that they were Gods.
But instead they found out it was *"The Devil"*.
That sail on that boat that fateful day.

Was it a tragedy?
Did he die a heroic death?
Was he s hero as he is made out to be?
Or just a megalomaniac seeking power & wealth.
Intent on the exploitation of Indigenous cultures.
To feed his greed, arrogance & sense of superiority & entitlement.
Because he had the shot gun.
Might is always right when you're holding a gun!
And your adversary is holding a stick or a rock!

Cook was a killer!
Let's bring down his statues.
Let's say how it was.
Let's not idolise him.
Like the *"White"* people do.
Let's state the facts.
Cook was a killer & that is a fact!

Cook Was a Killer

(Terra Nullis)

"The Don"
03.07.2020

Cook's map of the east coast of New South Wales, 1770

Cook's landing at Botany Bay

"Always Was, Always Will Be"
Artist: Kathyrn Dodd Farrow

"Uluru-Sacred Rock"
Artist: "Onya Monya"

Questions

Why are we cruel?
Why are we mean?
Why are we angry?
Why are we violent?
Why are there laws?
Why are there leaders?
Why are there politicians?
Why are there governments?
Why are there borders?
Why are there countries?
Why are there Nations?
Why are the wars!
Why are we born?

Why is there poverty?
Why is there discrimination?
Why is there exploitation?
Why is there jealousy?
Why is there greed?
Why is there money?
Why is there rich & poor?
Why is there bigotry?
Why is there prejudice?
Why is there hatred.
Why is there violence?
Why is there fear?
Why is there cruelty?
Why is there meanness?

Why do we work?
Why do we hate?
Why do we age?
Why do we lie?
Why do we die?

Why do we have leaders?
Why do we have monarchies?
Why do we have dictators?
Why do we have police?
Why do we have guns?
Why do we have weapons?
Why do we have "Weapons of Mass Destruction"?
Why do we have churches?
Why do we have religions?
Why do we have sin?
Why do we have guilt?
Why do we have the Devil?
Why do we have a God?
Why do we have homelessness?

Why don't we care?
Why don't we care for our environment?
Why don't we care for our planet?
Why don't we care for each other?
Why don't we give?
Why don't we have morals?
Why don't we have principles?
Why don't we live forever?
Why don't we Lo♥e more?
Why don't we get any answers?
Why don't we ask more questions?

#

"The Don"
04.07.2020

The Twilight Zone

The moment between today & tomorrow.
The space between yesterday & today.
That instant between day & night.
That realm between awake & sleep.
That line between reality & dreams.
That bridge between dreams & nightmares.
That moment between Life & Death.
That is The Twilight Zone.

When things just don't seem right.
When things are not what they seem
When things don't feel as they should.
When things suddenly have a different light.
When things suddenly have a new meaning.
When things are no longer normal.
When things are out of place.
You have just entered The Twilight Zone.

When you no longer recognise people you used to know.
When you don't know where you are.
When you been here before.
When you think you recognise a complete stranger.
When you don't feel like yourself.
When you don't know who you are.
When you don't recognise your reflection in the mirror.
You are in The Twilight Zone.

Expect the unexpected.
See the unknown.
Feel what you have never felt.
Think what you have never thought.
Imagine the unimaginable.
Believe the unbelievable.
Experience eternity.
This is The Twilight Zone.

If you can see your future.
If you can go back to your past.
If you can make your dreams become reality.
If you can communicate your thoughts.
If you imagine infinity.
If you can live forever.
If you can see you own Death
You living in The Twilight Zone.

If you know who Rod Serling was.
If you recognise these words.

"There is a fifth dimension beyond that which is known to man.
It is a dimension as vast as space and as timeless as infinity.
It is the middle ground between light and shadow, between science and superstition,
and it lies between the pit of man's fears
and the summit of his knowledge.
This is the dimension of imagination.
It is an area which we call The Twilight Zone."

"You're traveling through another dimension, a dimension not only of sight and sound but of mind.
A journey into a wondrous land whose boundaries are that of imagination.
That's the signpost up ahead—
your next stop, the Twilight Zone!"

"You unlock this door with the key of imagination.
Beyond it is another dimension—
a dimension of sound, a dimension of sight, a dimension of mind.
You're moving into a land of both shadow and substance, of things and ideas.
You've just crossed over into the Twilight Zone."

"The Don"
05.06.2020

Space, the Final Frontier

*"Space, the final frontier.
These are the voyages of the Starship Enterprise.
Its five year mission.
To explore strange new worlds.
To seek out new life.
And new civilizations.
To boldly go where no man has gone before!"*

When Neil Armstrong spoke those immortal words.
"That's one small step for man.
One giant leap for mankind."
As he took his first to be the first man to walk on the moon.
His footprints are still there.
There is no wind on the moon.
There is no atmosphere.

When JFK declared back in 1962.
*"We choose to go to the Moon.
We choose to go to the Moon...
We choose to go to the Moon in this decade
and do the other things,
not because they are easy,
but because they are hard;
because that goal will serve to organize and measure the best of our energies and skills,
because that challenge is one that we are willing to accept,
one we are unwilling to postpone, and one we intend to win, and the others, too."*

Where is this vision today?
Why are we not in Space!
Why don't we have a colony in the Moon?
Why have we lost our desire for exploration?
Why have we lost our need for adventure?
Why have we lost our curiosity?
Why have we lost our thirst for discovery?

Where has our imagination gone?
Where has the inspiration gone?
Where has it all gone?

Space, the Final Frontier is still there.
It is still waiting.
When will we finally break the shackles that bind us down?
Imprisoning us on Planet Earth.
Isn't it time to leave our home?
Isn't it time to make our way into the Universe?
Isn't it time to start our journey in Space, the Final Frontier?

"The Don"
05.07.2020

The Manhattan Project

It was in Los Alamos, New Mexico.
A *"top secret"* project was taking place.
It was 1940 in the middle of World War II.
There was something taking place.
Nobody was allowed to know what it was.
Because it could destroy the Human Race.
To obtain unimaginable power was their aim.
A power so great, only a God could obtain.

This was their aim.
This was their quest.
To find the Holy Grail.
To unlock the power of the atom.
To hold this power in man's hands.

His name was *Robert Oppenheimer*.
Leader of *"The Manhattan Project"*.
His mission, to make the first atomic bomb.
Before the Germans.
It was a race to destruction.
The destruction of the Human Race.
And possibly everything else.
Even the very planet itself.

They had no idea.
They had no clue.
What they were playing with.
What the destruction it could do.
They were blinded by science.
Or something even more sinister.
I don't really know?
But I know what they did.

The consequences were enormous.
Even *"Biblical"*, one might say.
They changed the world forever.
On that fateful day.
The word never be the same again.
The dragon had been unleashed.
To breathe out its awesome fire.
And leave the Earth scorched forever.

That day was *August 6th 1945*.
At *8:15am (Pacific Time)* in the morning.
The first atomic bomb was released.
It was dropped onto the city of Hiroshima.
In the country of Japan.
It instantly obliterated *one hundred thousand* people.
Innocent victims, not knowing what was about to happen.

Vapourised in a split second.
Disappearing forever.
Nothing ever to be found.
They were atomised.
Scattered in the wind.
A wind full of evil.
Contaminating the sky & land.
A poisonous wind carrying radiation on its wings.
Killing people years later.
Causing cancers & other hideous deformities.

Oppenheimer instantly realised what he had done.
Realised what he had become.
He was not a *"God"*, as he might have thought.
Instead he saw who he really was.
When he saw the destruction that he had brought.
He shouted in horror at the demon he had unleashed.
"I am Death, Destroyer of Worlds!", he said.
He was in fact, *"The Devil"*!

"The Don"
05.07.2020

Detail from the quilt
"It Depends on What grows in Your Garden"
By Mariclaire Pringle

The Cosmos

It's unimaginable.
It's unfathomable.
It's unbelievable.
It's unreal.
It's unseeable.
It's undreamable.
It's unthinkable.
It's unscrupulous.
It's unchallengeable.
It's unrelatable.
It's unconditional.
It's uncontrollable.
It's unintelligible.
It's uncontaminated.
It's undeniable.
It's unavailable.
It's uncooperative.
It's uncompromising.
It's unequivocal.

It's beyond thought.
It's beyond belief.
It's beyond imagination.
It's beyond our reach.
It's beyond creation.

It's extraordinary.
It's otherworldly.
It's out of this world.
It's surreal.
It's incredible.
It's indescribable.
It's indestructible.
It's inconceivable.
It's inconvenient.
It's inaccessible.

It's everything & nothing.
It's light & dark.
It's the "Big Bang".
It's the "Stairway to Heaven".
In fact, it IS Heaven.

It's mind-blowing.
It's our destination.
It's our Home.
It's where we come from.
It's where we go back to.

"The Don"
06.07.2020

Nemesis

You are not my enemy.
You are not my foe.
You are not my competitor.
You are not my competition.
You are not my opposer.
You are not my opposition.

We are not at war.
We are not at conflict.
We are not fighting.
We are not battling.
We are not in a race.
We are not enemies.

We are on the same side.
We are playing the same game.
We are having the same end.
We are brothers in arms.
We are playing the same tune.
We are singing the same song.

I am your friend.
I am on your side.
I am on your path.
I am with you all the way.
I am here to stay.
I am not your Nemesis.

"The Don"
07.07.2020

Perseverance

(Persévérance)

Perseverance is the key.
Perseverance opens every door.
Perseverance to never give up.
Perseverance to never give in.
Perseverance to "never say never!"
Perseverance to never stop.
Perseverance to never quit.
Perseverance to not give up the fight.
Perseverance to not throw in the towel.
Perseverance to not finish the race.
Perseverance to give it your best.
Perseverance to believe in yourself.
Perseverance to say, "I can do this".
Perseverance to the test.
Perseverance to the end.
Perseverance to go round again.
Perseverance to never drop.
Perseverance to reach your goal.
Perseverance to reach your Destiny.

Perseverance until you have no more to give.
Perseverance until all your fuel is exhausted.
Perseverance until there's no more fuel in your tank.
Perseverance until someone comes knocking at your door.
Perseverance until you get a tap on your shoulder.
Perseverance until you've taken your last breath.
Perseverance until your Death.

Persévérance

(Perseverance)

"The Don"
07.07.2020

Numerology

Do you believe in fate?
Do you believe in destiny?
Do you believe patterns?
Do you believe in a "Grand Design"?
Do you believe in "Cosmic Forces"?

Do you see patterns in Nature?
Do you see numbers everywhere?
Do you see beyond there is?
Do you see a deeper meaning?
Do you see a hidden truth?
Do you see "The Meaning"?

Do you have a key?
Do you have map?
Do you have compass?
Do you have a path?
Do you have a "Knowledge"?
Do you have an "Answer"?

Do you seek the "Mystical Forces"?
Do you seek the "Divine"?
Do you seek the "Answers"?
Do you seek to reach the "Stars"?
Do you seek to predict the "Future"?
Do you seek to predict your fate?

Do you like to play with numbers?
Do you like to play with number patterns?
Do you like to play with "Astrology"?
Do you like to play with the "Paranormal"?
Do you like to play with "Mystical Relationships"?
Do you like to play with "Numerology"?

"The Don"
07.07.2020

The Power of the Atom

Everything is made of atoms.
Unless of course it is energy.
They are in fact one & the same thing.
Einstein proved that.
With his equation, "$E=mc^2$".
Where "E" is Energy.
"m" is mass.
And "c" is the speed of light.

What this equation tells us is.
That matter is energy that has been slowed down & coalesced.
What that means is that, the energy is still there.
Locked up in the atom.

The power of the atom is in the nucleus.
This is where the "Protons" & "Neutrons" are located.
If the "Nucleus" is split.
Unimaginable power is released.
This is atomic energy.

But there are enormous risks involved.
With the release of awesome power comes with it, enormous dangers.
They go hand in hand.
You can't have one without the other.

Have you heard of "Alpha Particles"?
Have you heard of "Beta Rays"?
Have you heard of " Gamma Rays"?
I'm sure you have.
They were very popular in the 1950s & 60s Sci Fi films.

These are released during a "Nuclear explosion".
These make up what is called "radiation".
They all very dangerous.
But the most dangerous is the "Gamma ray".

Why?

Because it can penetrate through everything.
Even concrete & lead.
And it lasts for hundreds of thousands of years.
Once released into the atmosphere it travels in the wind.
Being absorbed into everything.

"Why is it so dangerous?", I hear you ask.
It is extremely dangerous because it can enter the cells of our body.
It can modify our DNA.
Causing cells to mutate.
This mutation is called "Cancer"!

They can any cell in our body.
Rearranging a "Genetic Code".
Our body has no defence for it.
It was never designed to be exposed.
To the high levels released in a "Nuclear explosion".

The mutations may not appear immediately.
They may take their time.
But your cells will never be the same.
If you are exposed a high level of "radiation".

From the first atomic explosion, called "Trinity".
Which took place in Los Alamos, New Mexico on 16th July, 1945
Hiroshima, Japan on 6th August 1945.
Nagasaki, Japan on 9th August 1945.
"Operation Buffalo" by the British in South Australia, between 1957 & 1963.
The French from 1960 to 1996 at Mururoa atoll, French Polynesia in the South Pacific.
The Three Mile Island, nuclear power plant accident on 28th March 1979 in Pennsylvania, USA.
The Chernobyl nuclear power plant accident on 26th April, 1986 in the Ukrainian.
The Fukushima nuclear power plant accident on 11th March, 2011 in Japan.
And all the other nuclear power tests that have been carried out not mentioned.
So much radiation has been released into the atmosphere throughout these years
Little wonder the incidence of cancers has gone rampant.

The point of this history lesson.
The moral of this story.
Is to learn from history.
To understand the science.
That there is no safe use for nuclear power.
There is no safe level of exposure to radiation.
Do not be fooled by politicians.
For their own agendas, to believe otherwise.
The power of the atom is something not to be taken lightly.

"The Don"
07.07.2020

Fire

(Fuoco)

Fire in your eyes.
Fire in your hands.
Fire in your feet.
Fire in your skin.
Fire in your belly.
Fire in your heart.
Fire in your brain.
Fire in your mind.
Fire in your movements.
Fire in your actions.
Fire in your thoughts.
Fire in your feelings.
Fire in your passion.
Fire in your desire.
Fire in your imagination.
Fire in your creativity.
Fire in your soul.
Fire in your Lo♥e.
Fire in your Life.
Fire in your Death.

Fire to burn FOREVER.

Burn, baby, BURN!

I'm on Fire!

"The Don"
08.07.2020

Pleasure & Pain
(Piacere e dolore)

One person's pleasure is another person's pain.
One person's day is another person's night.
One person's sun is another person's rain.
One person's happiness is another person's sadness.
One person's tears is another person's laughter.
One person's freedom is another person's prison.
One person's beauty is another person's Ugliness.
One person's trash is another person's treasure.
One person's wealth is another person's poverty.
One person's Intelligence is another person's stupidity.
One person's Future is another person's Past.
One person's today is another person's yesterday.
One person's male is another person's female.
One person's positive is another person's negative.
One person's reality is another person's illusion.
One person's white is another person's black.
One person's sweetness is another person's bitterness.
One person's sugar is another person's salt.
One person's thought is another person's thoughtlessness.
One person's positivity is another person's negativity.
One person's North is another person's South.
One person's cold is another person's hot.
One person's music is another person's noise.
One person's voice is another person's scream.
One person's eyes is another person's blindness.
One person's ears is another person's deafness.
One person's sexiness is another person's disgust.
One person's humility is another person's arrogance.
One person's frailty is another person's strength.
One person's strength is another person's weakness.
One person's bravery is another person's cowardice.
One person's kindness is another person's creulty.
One person's bravardo is another person's shyness.
One person's "Truth" is another person's "Lie".

One person's security is another person's insecurity.
One person's belief is another person's disbelief.
One person's smile is another person's sneer.
One person's protest is another person's subversion.
One person's law is another person's lawlessness.
One person's anarchy is another person's order.
One person's order is another person's disorder.
One person's science is another person's religion.
One person's home is another person's goal.
One person's "natural" is another person's "unnatural".
One person's sanity is another person's insanity.
One person's madness is another person's sanity.
One person's crazy is another person's normal.
One person's "Normal" is another person's "Abnormal".
One person's chaos is another person's order.
One person's society is another person's fragmentation.
One person's silence is another person's noise.
One person's loudness is another person's silence.
One person's respect is another person's disrespect.
One person's good is another person's bad.
One person's alone is another person's crowd.
One person's social is another person's unsocial.
One person's friendly is another person's unfriendly.
One person's enemy is another person's friend.
One person's poor is another person's rich.
One person's healthy is another person's sick.
One person's mind is another person's mindless.
One person's care is another person's careless.
One person's order is another person's disorder.
One person's security is another person's insecurity.
One person's political is another person's apolitical.
One person's something is another person's nothing.
One person's meaning is another person's meaningless.
One person's Heaven is another person's Hell.
One person's Lo♥e is another person's Hate.
One person's God is another person's Devil.
One person's Death is another person's Life.

"The Don"
08.07.2020

Namaste

Peace out.
Lo♥e out.
Joy out.
Happiness out.
Positivity out.
Humanity out.
Force out.
Light out.
Beauty out.
Health out.
Caring out.
Sunshine out.
Luck out.
Soul out.
Heart out.
Life out.
Greatness out.
Humility out.
Being out.
Faith out.
Purity out.
Enlightenment out.
Consciousness out.
Mindfulness out.
Thoughtfulness out.
Oneness out.
Togetherness out.
Unity out.
Community out.
Solidarity out.
Respect out.

I give to you Namaste out.

"The Don"
09.07.2020

Operation Buffalo

(Maralinga)

In Maralinga, South Australia.
A land that belonged to First Nation Peoples.
They lived on this land.
But the Australian Government lied.
The British Government secretly with the acknowledgment & support of the Australian Government of time.
It Conducted *"Nuclear tests"* between 1956 & 1963.

"Operation Buffalo" was conducted in 1956.
It consisted of 4 tests.
"Operation Antler" was conducted the following year.
It consisted of 3 tests.

It lied that no lived there.
It lied that it was completely empty.
It lied that it was lifeless.
It lied that it was safe.
It lied to its people.
It lied to the world.

It was a conspiracy.
Between the British & the Australian Governments.
Especially *"Sir Robert Menzies"*, Prime Minister at the time.
He was a nasty piece of work.
He introduced *"The White Australia Policy"*.
He started *"The Liberal Party"*.
He even stole the word "Liberal".
Redefined for his needs.
Redefined it to mean *"Conservative"*.

He was in power for 23 years.
His love for the Queen immense.
He said, *"I did but see her passing by & yet I will love her till I die."*
A monarchist to his very being.

He lied to his Parliamentary Cabinet.
He lied to the Australian people.
He lied to 1st Nations people.
He lied to the World.

There were 1st Nations People living there.
It was the home of the *"Maralinga Tjarutja"*, a southern *"Pitjantjatjara people"*.
The radiation was carried by the wind.
The land is uninhabitable for thousands of years to come.
They carried tests on humans.
They carried out tests on children & babies.
They cut off their limbs.
They dissected them like *"lab-rats"*.
They studied their exposure to radiation.
They were evil people.

The aim was to prepare for a *"Nuclear War"*.
To see the effects of radiation.

On humans.
On animals.
On the weather.
On the land.
On the plants.

They were immortal.
They were evil.
They were monsters.
They were an abomination of man.

Looking back, it makes me sad.
Looking back, it makes me angry.
Looking back, it makes me wanna cry.

At the cruelty of man!

"The Don"
09.07.2020

Map of Australia showing the area of the Maralinga Nuclear testing site in South Australia

Landscape of Maralinga Site

How to Make Relationships Work

Start with a lotta Lo♥e.
But that ain't enough.
That's just the beginning.
You need much, much more.
You will need a lot of elbow grease.
So, roll up your sleeves.
You got some baking to do.
Preheat the oven.
4,000 degrees should do.

Grease a large baking pan.
The largest one you've got.
With lots of friendship.
You don't want your relationships.
To stick to the bottom or the sides.

Into a bowl, these are the ingredients that you will need.
Don't be skimpy.
You will need a lot.

Take a lot of kindness.
The more you add the better.
Now, add a bucketful of cooperation.
And then, add copious amounts of compassion.
Finally, for the most important ingredient of all.

Respect.

I know it's expensive.
I know it's hard to find.
Though, all good people will have it.
Even if it's hidden, deep inside.
If you ask nicely.
I'm sure they'll look around.

It might be covered in dust.
Maybe a little bit mouldy.
But that won't matter much.
It won't affect the taste at all.
Respect doesn't have a "used by date".
Respect never goes off!

Now comes the hard part.
Mixing all these ingredients well.
It's gonna take a lot of hard work.
Are you prepared to put in the effort?

You gotta keep on mixing.
Until the mixture is all nice a smooth.
There can't be any lumpy bits.
It's gotta be very runny.
With a golden sheen.
Keep on stirring well.
Don't stop.
Don't run away.
If you want your relationships to work.

When you are satisfied that mixing has been.
It's blended to your satisfaction.
And your exhausted.
Now it's time for some fun.
But your work is never done!

Place the mixture into the greased baking pan.
Place the pan into the oven.
Put the timer on for "whenever".
Let it cook away.

Now, you can now walk away.
Though don't go too far.
Knowing that you'll be having the best relationship you've EVER tasted.
However, come & check on it.
Every now & then.
You don't want to overcook it.
You don't want to let it burn.

So, this is the secret.
Now you know.
It's actually, no a secret after all.
Unlike KFC's, 11 secret herbs & spices.
You can tell everyone about….
How to make relationships work.

"The Don"
10.07.2020

GFE

(Girlfriend Experience)

Wanna get a girlfriend!
Without all the strings attached.
$250 per hour is the starting rate.
Cash payment upfront.
And you're off on a date.

It's so easy.
Anyone can do it.
No application forms.
Or tests to pass.
Just pay up.
And you're on your way.

No need for romancing.
And all that fake *"love talk"*.
Just be yourself.
No need to pretend to be someone else.

Let your money do the talking.
Remember, *"Money doesn't talk, it swears!"*
You can buy anything you need.
You can buy whatever you desire.
Your pleasure is guaranteed!

She is a professional.
She knows just what to do.
She's done it all before.
This is nothing new.
Lay back & enjoy the ride.
Your hour will soon be over.
And you'll think that you've died & gone to Heaven.
When your ride is through.

So, whenever you're feeling lonely
Whenever you're feeling down.
Whenever you need a little bit of *"TLC"*.
Whenever you have the need for a girlfriend.
But don't want her to hang around.
Get yourself a GFE & everything will be great.

"The Don"
10.07.2020

Lo♥e In A Cold Climate
(Amore in un Clima Freddo)

Do you want some good Lo♥in'?
Do you wanna have some fun?
Do you wanna be held tight?
Do you wanna be told everything's gonna be alright.
Do you wanna make Lo♥e with the little lights on?
Do you wanna "bang-a-gong"?
Do you wanna sing a beautiful Lo♥e song?
Do you want make Lo♥e in a cold climate?

The best sorta Lo♥e is when it's raining.
The best sorta Lo♥e is when it's misty.
The best sorta Lo♥e is when it's foggy.
The best sorta Lo♥e is when it's windy.
The best sorta Lo♥e is when the wind is whistling through the trees.
The best sorta Lo♥e is when it's windy & cold.
The best sorta Lo♥e is when it's bitterly cold.
The best sorta Lo♥e is when it's snowing.
The best sorta Lo♥e is in a cold climate.

Let's snuggle up in front of the fire.
Let's get cosy like 2 bugs in a rug.
Let's roast marshmallows & drink hot chocolate.
Let's get naked a hold each tight.
Let's make Lo♥e until the fire goes out.
Let's stay up & watch the sunrise.
Let's have breakfast in bed.
Let's stay in bed all day, what ya' say?
Let's make Lo♥e in a cold climate.

Cold is warm.
Cold is cool.
Cold is fun.
Cold is food.
Cold is beautiful.
Cold is true.
Cold is goosebumps.
Cold is snug.
Cold is intimicy.
Cold is Lustful.
Cold is Soulful.
Cold is Life!
Cold is Lo♥e.
Lo♥e In A Cold Climate.

"I've NEVER felt so alive!"
When I make Lo♥e In A Cold Climate.

"The Don"
11.07.2020

Born to be Wild

You were born to be a rebel.
You were born to be a radical.
You were born to be an anarchist.
You were born to be fearless.
You were born to be brave.
You were born to be wild.
You were born to be a wild child.
You were born to be wild.

You have no fear.
You have no doubts
You have no illusions.
You have no insecurities.
You have no regrets.
You have no delusions.
You have no guilt.
You have no pain.
You have no despair.
You were born to be wild.

You are brave.
You are strong.
You are Noble.
You are fearless.
You are kind.
You are caring.
You are moral.
You are righteous.
You are never wrong.
You are born to be wild.

You are a leader.
You are a "Force of Nature".
You are a fighter.
You are a bearer of the "Light".
You are a "go getter".
You are a hero.
You are born to be wild.

You never take a backward step.
You never give up.
You never back down.
You never say "Never".
You never stop.
You never quit.
You never let anyone down.
You never break your word.
You never lie.
You were born to be wild.

You always tell the "Truth", no matter the cost.
You always move on.
You always follow your path.
You always follow your Destiny.
You always follow you Heart.
You always believe in yourself.
You always right for what is right.
You always fight injustices.
You always seek the "Truth".
You always work for "Justice".
You were born to be wild.

Born to be Wild

"The Don"
11.07.2020

Lo♥e?

(Amore)

Bob Dylan said that *"Lo♥e is just a four letter word"*.
Pat Benatar said that, *" Lo♥e is a battlefield"*.
Bryan Ferry said that, *" Lo♥e is the drug"*.
Hot Chocolate said that, *" Lo♥e is in the backseat of my Cadillac"*.
John Paul Young said that, *"Lo♥e is in the air"*.
Foreigner said, *"I want to know what Lo♥e is"*.
The Beatles said that, *"All you need Lo♥e "*.
And that, you *"Can't buy me Lo♥e "*.
Leonard Cohen said, *"Dance me to the end of Lo♥e "*.

Lo♥e is feeling.
Lo♥e is caring.
Lo♥e is kindness.
Lo♥e is compassion.
Lo♥e is selfless.
Lo♥e is nurturing.
Lo♥e is freedom.
Lo♥e e is respect.
Lo♥e is dispossession.
Lo♥e is oneness.
Lo♥e is Nature.
Lo♥e is intelligence.
Lo♥e is spiritual.
Lo♥e is universal.
Lo♥e is cosmic.
Lo♥e is humble.
Lo♥e is humility.
Lo♥e is human.

Lo♥e never runs out.
Lo♥e never dies.
Lo♥e never is too much.
Lo♥e never destroys.
Lo♥e never is violent.
Lo♥e never is abusive.
Lo♥e never is jealous.
Lo♥e never is possessive.
Lo♥e never is arrogant.
Lo♥e never is inhumane.
Lo♥e never is inhuman.

Lo♥e is NOT just a four letter word.

"The Don"
12.07.2020

Pussy Power

Girl Power.
Grrrrrrrrl Power.
GRRRRRRRRRL POWER.
Woman Power.
Womin Power.
Women Power.
Wimin Power.
Herstory.
HerStory.
Huwoman.
Huwomin.
Huwimin.
Huwomanity.
Huwominity.
Huwiminity.
Warrior Woman.
Warrior Womin.
Warrior Wimin.
Go Girl.
Go Grrrrrrrrl.
Go GRRRRRRRL.
GRRRRRRRRROWL.

Pussy to Power.
Pussies to Power.
Pussy Power.

"Sisters are doin' it for themselves"

Now there was a time when they used to say
That behind every - great man.
There had to be a - great woman.
But in these times of change you know
That it's no longer true.
So, we're comin' out of the kitchen
'Cause there's somethin' we forgot to say to you (we say)

Sisters are doin' it for themselves.
Standin' on their own two feet.

Sisters are doin' it for themselves.
Standin' on their own two feet.

And ringin' on their own bells.
Sisters are doin' it for themselves.

Now this is a song to celebrate
The conscious liberation of the female state!
Mothers, daughters and their daughters too.
Woman to woman
We're singin' with you.
The inferior sex got a new exterior
We got doctors, lawyers, politicians too.
Everybody, take a look around.
Can you see, can you see, can you see
There's a woman right next to you.
Sisters are doin' it for themselves.

Standin' on their own two feet.
And ringin' on their own bells.
Sisters are doin' it for themselves.
Now we ain't makin' stories
And we ain't layin' plans
'cause a man still loves a woman
And a woman still loves a man
(just a same though).

Songwriters: Annie Lennox/Dave Stewart

"I am woman"

I am woman, hear me roar
In numbers too big to ignore
And I know too much to go back an' pretend
'Cause I've heard it all before
And I've been down there on the floor
No one's ever gonna keep me down again
Oh yes, I am wise
But its wisdom born of pain
Yes, I've paid the price
But look how much I gained
If I have to, I can do anything

I am strong (Strong)
I am invincible (Invincible)
I am woman

You can bend but never break me
'Cause it only serves to make me
More determined to achieve my final goal
And I come back even stronger
Not a novice any longer
'Cause you've deepened the conviction in my soul
Oh yes, I am wise
But its wisdom born of pain
Yes, I've paid the price
But look how much I gained
If I have to, I can do anything

I am strong (Strong)
I am invincible (Invincible)
I am woman

I am woman watch me grow
See me standing toe to toe
As I spread my lovin' arms across the land
But I'm still an embryo
With a long, long way to go
Until I make my brother understand
Oh yes, I am wise
But its wisdom born of pain
Yes, I've paid the price
But look how much I gained
If I have to, I can face anything

I am strong (Strong)
I am invincible (Invincible)
I am woman

I am woman
I am invincible
I am strong
I am woman
I am invincible
I am strong
I am invincible
I am strong
I am woman.

Songwriters: Helen Reddy/Ray Burton

"The Don",
13.07.2020

Thinking

(Pensiero)

Thinking causes stress.
Thinking causes pain.
Thinking causes nightmares.
Thinking causes problems.
Thinking causes unhappiness.
Thinking causes sadness.
Thinking causes loneliness.
Thinking causes sorrow.
Thinking causes heartache.
Thinking causes futility.
Thinking causes despair.
Thinking causes disappointment.
Thinking causes disillusionment.
Thinking causes disunity.
Thinking causes disharmony.
Thinking causes social unrest.
Thinking causes rebellion.
Thinking causes opposition.
Thinking causes unease.
Thinking causes questioning.
Thinking causes reasoning.
Thinking causes debate.
Thinking causes conversation.
Thinking causes social interaction.
Thinking causes Intelligence.
Thinking causes solutions.
Thinking causes creativity.
Thinking causes instability.
Thinking causes revolution.
Thinking causes disruption.
Thinking causes social unrest.

Thinking HURTS!

Please, Do NOT think!

"The Don"
14.07.2020

Black Beauty

She's as wise as the Land.
She's as kind as the air.
She's as old as the stars.
She's as warm as The Sun.
She's as bright as The Moon.
She's as shy as summer breeze.
She's as cuddly as a Koala.
She's as creative as Nature.
She's as loyal as the sea.
She's as knowledgeable as the trees.
She's as strong as a rock.
She's as free as the wind.
She's as beautiful as a rainforest.
She's as deep as an ocean.
She's as powerful as a river.
She's as cute as a "Gumnut Baby".
She's delicious as bush tucker.
She's as tasty as food from "Lillipad Café".
She's as smart as dolphin.
She's as colourful as "The Great Barrier Reef".
She's as beautiful as a snowflake.
She's as delicate as rose.
She's as powerful as a cyclone.
She's as fragile as The Earth.
She's as immense as The Universe.
She's as soulful as whale.
She's as silent as blank page.
She's as loud as thunder.
She's as electric as lightning.
She's as sacred as Uluru.
She's as mysterious as "Yowie Woman".
She's as humane as a human should be.

She's the "Black Queen of Glebe".

"The Don"
15.07.2020

Nose Bleed

*"We all need someone we can bleed on.
And if you wanna?
You can bleed on me."*

I *bleed* for the lonely.
I *bleed* for the weak.
I *bleed* for the sick.
I *bleed* for the unhappy.
I *bleed* for the unwanted.
I *bleed* for the unloved.
I *bleed* for the homeless.
I *bleed* for the abused.
I *bleed* for the discriminated.
I *bleed* for the dispossessed.
I *bleed* for the oppressed.
I *bleed* for the injustices.
I *bleed* for the loss of youth.
I *bleed* for the old.
I *bleed* for the young.
I *bleed* for the poor.
I *bleed* for the rich......*NOT*!
I *bleed* for the environment.
I *bleed* for the Future.
I *bleed* for the Past.
I *bleed* for the destruction.
I *bleed* for the voiceless.
I *bleed* for the unheard.
I *bleed* for Humanity
I *bleed* for the dying.
I *bleed* for the Dead.

I bleed for you.

"The Don"
16.07.2020

Subjectivity

What is beautiful?
What is beauty?
What is ugly?
What is good?
What is bad?
What is naughty?
What is nice?
What is nasty?
What is sexy!
What is sexless?
What is art?
What is handsome?
What is right?
What is wrong!
What is truth?
What is lying?
What is deception?
What is funny?
What is serious?
What is history?
What is prejudice?
What is bias?
What is opinion?
What is fact?
What is true?
What is legal?
What is illegal?
What is "natural"?
What is "unnatural"?
What is "normal"?

What is "abnormal"?
What is "weird"?
What is "make believe"?
What is thought?
What is justice?
What is injustice?
What is sin?
What is holy?
What is unholy?
What is God?
What is The Devil.
What is "Reality"?
What is "Illusion"?
What is madness?
What is insanity?
What is sanity?
What is "Spirituality"?
What is "Real"?
What is "Unreal"?
What is male?
What is female?
What is "Lo♥e"?
What is "Hate"?
What is Death?
What is "After Death"?
What is Heaven?
What is Hell?
What is "Subjectivity?

"The Don"
17.07.2020

It's Not Either Or

It's not either or.
It's more, more, more.
It's not this or that.
It's both.
It's not you or him.
It's you & him
It's not you or her
It's yes to you & her
It's not either or.
It's yes to both.
It's not cream or icecream.
It's cream & icecream.
It's not one friend is enough.
It's one friend is not enough.
It's not one true lo♥e.
It's many true lo♥es.
It's not one night of bliss.
It's many nights of bliss.
It's not less is better.
It's more is better.
It's not less is more.
It's more is more.
It's not the glass half empty.
It's the glass half full.
It's not a life half lived.
It's a life fully lived.
It's not a life of emptiness & acceptance.
It's a life of fullness & adventure.
It's not a life of struggling & hardship.
It's a life of enjoyment & happiness.
It's not either or.
It's yes, more, more, more.

"The Don"
18.07.2020

Angry Poetry

(The Anti-Virus)

You got something to say?
You wanna get something off your mind?
Things are not going your way?
There's too many ups & downs.

Write it down.
Get it off your chest.
Let the whole world know about it.
Write some angry poetry to make yourself feel better.

The Future's looking bleak.
Fish are dying in the river.
"Lack of Oxygen" they say.
Heaven help us, I'm feeling weak.

There's pollution in the river.
"Fuck me, I just swam there the other day!"
It's just getting outta hand.
Everything seems to be going crazy.

Nothing seems to make any sense no more.
Please, someone help me see the door?
I don't know what to eat anymore.
Everything's fucked, I don't can't keep score.

Politicians say they have everything under control.
You must be joking man?
Are you living on another planet?
'Cause it sure doesn't look like that that from where I'm standing.

Disorder & chaos is reigning supreme.
No one knows what the fuck is going on.
There's a virus that's outta control.
It's killing everything in its path.

Fear & panic in people's eyes.
We're all waiting for a vaccine.
We're all waiting for a cure.
But will it work, no one's sure.

Fear & panic in people's eyes.
We're all waiting for a vaccine.
We're all waiting for a cure.
But will it work, no one's sure.

The economy's down the gurgler.
Unemployed rates are through the roof.
Stimulus packages being given out.
But I'm not feeling any better.

"Do this, don't that".
We're being micromanaged like never before.
"Stay indoors. Self-isolate!"
"Social distancing" is the "new norm".

Remember the "4 square metre rule".
But I was never taught that at school.
"Stay apart, one arm's length".
"Don't get too close, wear a mask".

How did this happen?
Who is too blame?
I don't remember doing anything wrong.
Yet, I know must play this crazy game.

There are no rules.
They're making them up as they go.
"What "Stage" are we in, I forgot?"
Maybe "Stage 2" or is it "Stage 3", I'm really not sure?"

There's virus going round & it's outta control.
It may already be too late to bring it back down.
No one knows for sure.
A month, two months, six months, maybe more.

It's smart & intelligent.
It has a mind of its own.
It's super adaptive & quick to replicate.
That virus' name is, "Homosapien"!

I have the solution.
I have the cure.
I have the "Anti-Virus".
Write "Angry Poetry" & let it ALL OUT!

"The Don"
19.07.2020

What is Life?

Is Life a joke?
Is Life a tragedy?
Is Life a comedy?
Is Life a journey?
Is Life an accident?
Is Life a mistake?
Is Life an aberration?
Is Life a "quirk of Nature"?
Is Life a burden?
Is Life a sufferance?
Is Life a punishment?
Is Life a prison sentence?
Is Life a disease?
Is Life a miracle?
Is Life a wonder?
Is Life a sin?
Is Life an illusion?
Is Life a dream?
Is Life a nightmare?
Is Life a "Matrix"?
Is Life a "Computer simulation"?
Is Life an "Algorithm"?
Is Life a "Mathematical equation"?
Is Life a "Reality"?
Is Life a "Living Hell"?
Is Life a mirage?
Is Life a "Dimension"?
Is Life a "Portal"?
Is Life a mystery?

Is Life meaningless?

What is Life?

"The Don"
19.07.2020

La Dolce Vita

(The Sweet Life)

Life is good.
Life is sweet.
Life is bliss.
Life is fun.
Life is great.
Life is neat.
Life is tasty.
Life is fruity.
Life is ripe.
Life is trippy.
Life is groovy.
Life is hard.
Life is heartless.
Life is worthless.
Life is priceless.
Life is a drug.
Life is a treat.
Life is a blast!
Life is a celebration.
Life is a party.
Life is full of surprises.
Life is a good time.
Life is a one-way trip.
Life is a piece of cake.
Life is a question.
Life is full of suffering.
Life is full of sorrow.
Life is full of Death.
Life is..........

"The Don"
19.07.2020

(I Want to be) Marcello Mastroianni

I want to be handsome.
I want to be sexy.
I want to be suave.
I want to be COOL.
I want to be HOT!
I want to be groovy
I want to be sophisticated.
I want to be attractive.
I want to be "drop dead gorgeous".
I want to be a "chick magnet".
I want to be enigmatic.
I want to be charismatic.
I want to be mysterious.
I want to be alluring.
I want to be unforgettable.
I want to be adorable.
I want to be desirable.
I want to be "sex on legs".
I want to be an "international man of mystery".
I want to be Rudolph Valentino
I want to be Casanova.
I want to be Don Juan.
I want to be Errol Flynn.
I want to be Cary Grant.
I want to be a young Marlon Brando.
I want to be a young Elvis Presley.
I want to be Paul Newman.
I want to be a young Al Pacino.
I want to be an older George Clooney.
I want to be Marcello Mastroianni.

I want to live in Rome.
I want to have a house on Lake Como.
I want to have "Free Love".
I want to smoke cigarettes like they did in the 1960s.
I want "La Dolce Vita".

I want to make Love to Anita Ekberg.
I want to make Love to Anouk Aimée.
I want to make Love to Nico.
I want to make Love to Sophia Loren.
I want to make Love to Claudia Cardinale.
I want to make Love to Ornella Muti.
I want to make Love to Marilyn Monroe.
I want to make Love to Jeanne Moreau.
I want to make Love to Candice Bergen.
I want to make Love to Barbarella.
I want to make Love to Charlotte Rambling.
I want to make Love to Julie Christie.
I want to make Love to Elizabeth Taylor.
I want to make Love to Dominique Sanda.
I want to make Love to Catherine Deneuve.
I want to make Love to Marianne Faithfull.
I want to make Love to Romy Schneider.
I want to make Love to Helen Miriam
I want to make Love to Silvia Kristel.
I want to make Love to Faye Dunaway.
I want to make Love to Monica Bellucci.
I want to make Love to Brigitte Bardot.
I want to make Love to Jane Fonda.
I want to make Love to Marie Schneider.
I want to make Love to Jennifer Lawrence.

I want to be Marcello Mastroianni.

"The Don"
21.07.2020

Rantings of a Madman
(Discorso di un Pazzo)

I've got things to say.
I've got things on my mind.
I've got things I regret
I've got things I gotta let out.

I've got things I gotta protest about.
I've got things I gotta sing about.
I've got things I gotta pray about.

I've got things I need to talk about.
I've got things I need to write down.

I've got things I'm happy about.
I've got things I'm ashamed about.
I've got things I'm angry about.
I've got things I'm not happy about.

I've got things I wanna do
I've got things I wanna see changed.
I've got things I wanna shout out about.
I've got things I wanna get off my chest.
I've got things I wanna scream about.
I've got things I wanna cry over.
I've got things I wanna laugh at.
I've got things I wanna punch.
I've got things I wanna jump up & down over.
I've got things I wanna die over.

I've got things that are not going my way.

I've got things that make me see "RED".
I've got things that make me feel bad.
I've got things that make me feel sad.
I've got things that make me cry.
I've got things that give me nightmares.
I've got things that make sweat.

I've got things I wish I'd never done.

I've got things..........

"The Don"
22.07.2020

Bottle of Wine

(Bottiglia di Vino)

Will it be a Shiraz?
"No thank you".
"A bit too heavy."
It was called "Claret" in the old days,
Wasn't it?"
How about a Cab Sav, then?
"Ah, a "Cabernet Sauvignon".
Oui, monsieur.
Yes, that's a good suggestion.
Everyone's favourite.
Not too heavy, not too light."

"Although, I do like a good "Merlot".
Lighter than a "Cab Sav".
A good alternative.
Especially, when there's going to be a lot of drinking to be done."
What about a "Rosé"?
"Oh, yes please but make sure it's a "Mateus".
Of course, sinore."

How about a Pinot Noir?
Chilled, of course.
"The only way to drink it.
Yes, thanks".

My favourite red wine is a "Tempranillo".
An often overlooked red from Spain.

How about some Champagne?
"If I'm going to have bubbles,
I think I'll have a "Prosceco".
Of course, one must have a Prosceco.
But one only from Italy, non?"
Si.

"Bottle of wine.
Fruit of the vine.
When are you gonna let me get sober?
Leave me alone.
Let me go home.
Let me go home
And start over."

"The Don"
22.07.2020

The Legend of
Jonah Lomou

Was it a bus?
Was it a train?
Was it a steamroller?
No!
It was Jonah Lomou.

He exploded onto the world scene at the Rugby World Cup in South Africa in 1995.
He was a winger for the NZ "All Blacks" team.
He was just 20 years old.
Off the field he was a "gentle giant".
On the field he was just a "giant".
He was a true "gentleman of the game".

It was the game against England.
He got the ball at the half way line.
One, two, three, four & finally only the English fullback, Mike Catt, was left.
Catt was brave, that's for sure.
He stood his ground.
That's all he could do.
Except, maybe run away.
But he was no match for the great Jonah Lomou.
Who ran right over the top of him.
Left him sprawled on his back.

"What the fuck just happened?".
He must've thought to himself.
Lomou had just scored the greatest try anyone had ever scene.
It was history in the making.
No one had ever seen a winger like him before.
No one has ever seen a number 11 like him ever since.

No one ever knew though.
That he played with an underlying medical condition.
He had a kindney disease.
But he didn't let that stop him.
In fact, it drove him to be his best on the field.
With his size, his speed & the power.
No one could stop him.
He was a true powerhouse.
Possibly, the greatest Rugby player of all time.

Jonah Lomou died of a heart attack on 18th November, 2015.
He was just 40 years old.
But he will never die.
He is an immortal now.
He will live forever.

On a lonely hilltop, in an Auckland cemetery.
There is an unmarked grave.
There is no headstone to identify who it is.
But all the locals know his name.
He died a pauper, with no money or wealth left to his name.
He was buried in a pauper's grave.
All the wealth & money that he had made was gone.
Maybe because he was a very kind, gentle hearted man.
Maybe, one day someone will put one up.
Maybe, that day will never come.
But I know & shall never forget who that man was.
For he was the great, Jonah Lomou.

If you don't know who Jonah Lomou is.
Do yourself a favour & look at these games.
The NZ "All Blacks" against the English "Lions".
And then, against the mighty SA "Springboks".
Even Nelson Mandela, who was there at the game.
Stood up & cheered for a player of the "other" side.
He had too.
Because the name of that player was, Jonah Lomou.

The Legend of
Jonah Lomou

"The Don"
23.07.2020

In the Garden of Eden
(In a Gadda da Vida)

There is innocence.
There is purity.
There is virginity.
There is Light.
There is frivolity.
There is fun.
There is nudity.
There is nakedness.
There is nudity.
There is beauty.
There is Nature.
There is a fig leaf.
There is flute music.
There is fruit.
There is whiteness.
There is sensuality.
There is naivety.
There is virtue.
There is righteousness.
There is decency.
There is morality.
There is chastity.
There is wholesomeness.
There is virtuousness.
There is temptation.
There is guilt.
There is Sin.
There is Desire.
There is immortality.
There is "Forbidden Fruit".
There is God.

"The Don"
23.07.2020

In the Garden of Perdition
(In a Gadda da Petition)

There is sex.
There is passion.
There is Pleasure.
There is nudity.
There is nakedness.
There is fun.
There is laughter.
There is humour.
There is "Rock & Roll" music.
There is Pain.
There is Suffering.
There is sorrow.
There is tomorrow.
There is Immorality.
There is dishonesty.
There is lying.
There is manipulation.
There is copulation.
There is fornication.
There is debauchery.
There is drunkenness.
There is treachery.
There is violence.
There is Lo♥e.
There is Hate.
There is destruction.
There is murder.
There is Evil.
There is Death.
There is the Devil.
There is Inhumanity.

"The Don"
25.07.2020

HerStory

WhoseStory?
WhichStory?
WhenStory?
WhereStory?
HowStory?
YesStory?
FemStory?
GirlStory?
WominStory?
WiminStory?
HumiliationStory?
AbusedStory?
UsedStory?
ExploitedStory?
DeniedStory?
HiddenStory?
RejectedStory?
SisterStory?
WifeStory?
HatedStory?
MistreatedStory?
RepeatedStory?
SharedStory?
SorryStory?
LifeStory?
NoStory?
NeverendingStory?
FutureStory?
PastStory?
ForeverStory?
MyStory?
BeautifulStory?
YesStory?
EmpowermentStory?
HuminStory?
HerStory!

"The Don"
23.07.2020

The Times They Are NOT A-Changin'

History always repeats.
We never learn from our mistakes.
Nothing will ever change.
No one listens anyhow.
No really care.
Money doesn't talk it swears.
Everything is fake anyway.
Everyone lies & that's the truth.
Violence is in our Nature.

We were born to be violent.
We don't know what Lo♥e is.
We don't know how to Lo♥e.
We know how to hate, though.
We know how to be angry.
We know how to be violent.

We never learn.
We never see.
Because we never look.
We don't listen.
Because we don't hear.
We don't feel.
Because our hearts are closed.

There are those among us who are *"Idealists"*.
Unfortunately, I am one of those.
I'd like to believe that *"a glass is half full rather than half empty"*.
Call us delusional.
Call us mad.
Call us crazy.
But it doesn't really matter.
'Cause things never change anyway.

Politicians keep on lying.
The rich keep on getting richer.
The poor keep on getting poorer.
Wars keep on happing.
People still keep getting exploited.
More laws erode our freedoms.
Discrimination is running rampant.
Human consciousness is diminishing.
People are getting more ignorant.
Although, there is more information available than ever before.
There is fake news.
In fact, everything is fake.

So, don't get upset.
Stay cool.
Nothing ever changes anyway.
For *"The Times They Are NOT A-Changin'"*.

"The Don"
24.07.2020

𝔇eath
is the 𝔓rice 𝔜ou 𝔓ay
for
𝔏iving

What is Death?

Is it Natural?
Is it Normal?
Is it necessary?
Is it needed?
Is it inevitable?
Is it part of the "Natural Order of Things"?
Is it in our DNA?
Is it "God's Will"?
Is it punishment?
Is it "planned obsolescence"?

Can we escape it?
Can we challenge it?
Can we change it?
Can we defy it?
Can we rebel against it?
Can we modify it?

Can we live forever?
Can we not die?
Or is death the price we pay for living?

"The Don"
24.07.2020

Books written by "The Don"

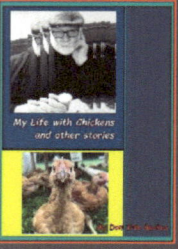

"My Life with Chickens & other stories: I Pity the Poor Immigrant"
Published:
10th September, 2019
Autobiography Book 1:
0 – 12 years old

"Poems for Misfits, Miscreants, Misanthropes, Mavericks, Losers & Malcontents!"
Published:
10th June, 2020
Book of Poems 1

"Poems for Troubled Minds & Trouble Hearts"
Published:
10th August, 2020
Book of Poems 2

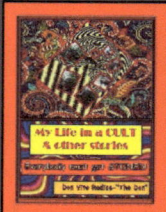

"My Life in a CULT & other stories: Everybody Must Get STONED!"
Published:
10th September, 2020
Autobiography Book 2:
15 – 30 years old

"Poems for Restless Minds & Restless Hearts"
Published:
10th October, 2020
Book of Poems 3

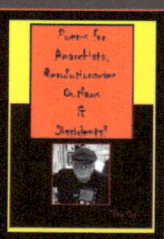

"Poems for Anarchists, Revolutionaries, Outlaws & Dissidents!"
Published:
10th November, 2020
Book of Poems 4

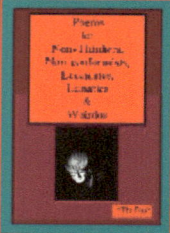

"Poems for Non-Thinkers & Eccentrics"
Published:
10th December, 2020
Book of Poems 5

"The Rantings of a Madman"
Published:
10th January, 2021
Book of Poems 6

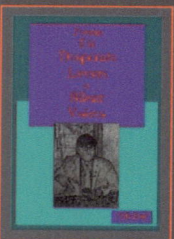

"Poems for Desperate Lovers & Silent Voices"
Published:
10th February, 2021
Book of Poems 7

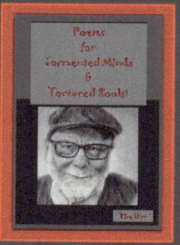

"Poems for Tormented Minds & Tortured Souls"
Published:
10th March, 2021
Book of Poems 8

All available ONLY online

www.ingramcontent.com/pod-product-compliance
Lightning Source LLC
Chambersburg PA
CBHW041502010526
44107CB00049B/1619